Dennis P. Smiley
July 15, 1975

Dennis P. Smiley
620 Airport Access Rd.
Apt. #8
Traverse City, Michigan 49684

Colourful Scotland

Colourful Scotland

Described by Alexander Rutherford

Jarrold & Sons Ltd

The Lowlands

The Lowlands of Scotland are generally considered to consist of the country south of the estuaries of the Forth and the Clyde, the lower regions of the eastern seaboard and the counties of Banffshire, Morayshire and Nairnshire. Yet the word 'lowland' in this context is a comparative term, for there are summits in the Lowlands which approach 2,500 feet. It is perhaps more satisfying to identify the Highlands with those areas where the population is predominantly of Gaelic-speaking Celtic origin and the Lowlands, as the rest of the country, but in the last analysis the distinction is merely one of geographical convenience and Scotland is certainly no divided country.

Of the four counties in the south-west, Wigtown and Kirkcudbrightshire bordering the Solway Firth once formed with the southern part of Ayrshire the ancient province of Galloway. Here agriculture and the raising of livestock are the principal rural occupations, and industry which once flourished in the small towns of Galloway now tends to be concentrated in the larger centres. Dumfriesshire extends from the English border into the mountains, from which long dales reach down to the sea. Ayrshire has a long coastline bordering the Clyde and a number of pleasant holiday resorts: it gave its name to the well-known breed of cattle, and dairy farming is of considerable importance. Robert Burns, Scotland's national poet, was born in 1759 in a humble cottage at Alloway, two miles south of Ayr. The cottage is now restored and refurnished in the style of the period, and a near-by museum houses relics of the poet.

There are also four Lowland counties in the south-east – Roxburgh, Berwick, Selkirk and Peebles. Roxburghshire is largely an upland county intersected by lovely dales, the most important being that of the Teviot. Ancient pele towers, the ruined abbeys of Jedburgh, Melrose and Kelso and fortified castles such as Hermitage, all bear witness to the long and often bitter struggles which once took place in the Border counties. Berwickshire owes its name to the town which is now in England. It lies between the Lammermuir Hills and the Tweed and includes the Merse, one of the most fertile areas in Scotland. Agriculture and fishing are the principal means of livelihood. There are only some twenty thousand people in the whole of Selkirkshire and all but three thousand live in Selkirk and Galashiels. The county is largely synonymous with Ettrick Forest and was once a royal hunting ground, but today a considerable area is devoted to the rearing of sheep and the woollen industry thrives. Peeblesshire, between Selkirkshire and Midlothian, is drained by the Tweed and its tributaries, a fact which endears the county to anglers. A surprising fact is that the mean altitude of Peeblesshire is greater than that of any other Scottish county. Like its neighbour to the south, Peeblesshire is sparsely populated, and once again the chief occupations of its inhabitants are agriculture and stock-raising.

As we move northwards towards the Clyde and the Forth the countryside gradually gives place to industrial development and the towns become larger and more numerous, yet only a short way from the sprawling metropolis of Glasgow there are considerable areas of natural beauty. Renfrewshire, which borders the Clyde, is a small but densely populated county with coal and iron mines, shipbuilding yards and both cotton and woollen manufacture. Lanarkshire stretches from Glasgow to the source of the Clyde. Although predominantly industrial it has famous orchards and thriving dairy-farming. The River Clyde is born in the extreme south of the county; its course has been dammed to supply electricity and a water supply for the district. Dunbartonshire, on the north bank of the Clyde, has many of the famous shipyards, but its western boundary passes through Loch Lomond and so the county reaches into the Highlands. Stirling, too, is partly a Highland county, although its northern boundary is the River Forth. In the troubled days of the Middle Ages when the English and Scots were often at war with each other, great battles were fought in Stirlingshire, including the Battles of Stirling Bridge, Falkirk and the most famous of all, Bannockburn, where Robert the Bruce defeated in 1314 the army of Edward II, in spite of the superior forces of the latter.

Six counties cradle the Firth of Forth. To the north are Fife, Clackmannanshire and Kinross, while south of the river are East Lothian, Midlothian and West Lothian. The latter form part of the former province of Lothian, which also included Roxburghshire and Berwickshire, and which was annexed by the Scots at the beginning of the eleventh century. West Lothian is partly industrial and almost half of Midlothian lies within the boundaries of Edinburgh. The north of East Lothian is particularly good agricultural land; in the south of the county are the Lammermuir Hills. Fife has the Tay Estuary on its northern flank and the Forth on its southern, with fine sandy beaches on its North Sea coast. Kinross is renowned for the beauty of Loch Leven beneath the Lomond Hills with some of the best fishing in Scotland. Clackmannanshire, Scotland's smallest county, has the Ochill Hills on its northern boundary with Kinross.

North of the estuary of the Tay the Lowlands extend in a continuous belt, broken in Perthshire and Angus by the Sidlaw Hills, with the sea on one side and the mountains on the other. North of Aberdeenshire the three counties of Banffshire, Morayshire and Nairnshire continue this area to the shores of the Moray Firth. Perth is the gateway to this region, as it is to the eastern Highlands. There is much historical interest, especially the numerous castles and fine old baronial houses, and both Dundee and Aberdeen are good centres from which to explore. Both Kincardineshire and Aberdeenshire have notable fishing ports, and the latter county is famous for its cattle, especially the black strain which originated in Angus. Both Banffshire and Morayshire have old-established whisky distilleries.

Edinburgh, the capital of Scotland, is both glorious and gracious; a city whose history lives in the Castle, the Palace of Holyrood, the Royal Mile and incomparable Princes Street, and Edinburgh even has a mountain within its boundaries – the 800-foot-high volcanic hill called 'Arthur's Seat' – from which a wonderful panorama of the city may be enjoyed. Until the eighteenth century the Old Town, to the south of the valley of the Nor' Loch, had been the focus of the life of the capital, but the construction of the North Bridge, a sloping viaduct spanning the valley, opened up the area to the north. The panorama of Princes Street (*above*) with Princes Street Gardens, the Scott Memorial and, dominating the scene, the Castle, is surely one of the most famous views in the British Isles and Princes Street is justly famous as one of Europe's finest thoroughfares. The Scott Monument was completed in 1844 and in the niches surrounding it are representations of figures from his works.

One of Edinburgh's most celebrated vantage points is Carlton Hill, with its vista of both the Old Town and the New (*upper right*). It was Stevenson who pointed out that this was the best place to view both the Castle and Arthur's Seat. Among the monuments on the hill are those to Lord Nelson and Dugald Stewart, the latter a copy of the 'Lantern of Demosthenes' at Athens.

Wherever you may go in Edinburgh, you are always conscious of the Castle (*lower right*) perched high above the town. The Castle has such a commanding position on the ridge where the Old Town is situated, that it is not surprising that its history was for long a succession of assaults and counter-assaults. Today the Castle leads a more peaceful existence as a military establishment.

Le jardin de Princes Street (*à gauche*) sépare l'Ancienne Ville de la Nouvelle: au fond le célèbre Château et à droite le monument en mémoire de Sir Walter Scott. Depuis Calton Hill (*ci-dessous, en haut*) on jouit d'une belle perspective sur Édimbourg. Sur l'Esplanade du Château (*ci-dessous, en bas*) a lieu tous les ans le « Tattoo », spectacle militaire qui attire nombreux spectateurs.

Die Anlagen von der Princes Street (*links*) befinden sich zwischen Alt- und Neustadt; links sieht man die bekannte Burg, rechts das Denkmal Sir Walter Scotts. Von Calton Hill (*unten*) aus hat man einen schönen Blick auf die Stadt Edinburg. Jedes Jahr bietet man im Burghof von Edinburg (*ganz unten*) das ,,Tattoo", ein militärisches Schauspiel, das Tausende von Zuschauern anzieht.

The Royal Mile, from the Castle to Holyrood, is the most historic street in the Old Town. The houses of many renowned Scots families were formerly situated in this part of the city, and some of the better-preserved buildings have been incorporated into a comprehensive scheme of reconstruction whose aim has been to restore the Royal Mile to its erstwhile glory. Among the buildings which have escaped the hand of time, three are particularly worthy of attention. The first is Canongate Tolbooth, an excellent example of the French architectural style which was fashionable at the end of the sixteenth century. The older part of the building was once the courthouse of the Burgh of the Canongate. The second is Moray House which dates from 1628 and has some fine rooms. Lastly there is the splendid timber-fronted Huntley House which once belonged to the 'Hammermen of Canongait'. The name 'Canongate' reminds us that this street was once used by the canons of the Abbey of St Augustine on their way to the Castle. At the bottom of Canongate is White Horse Close (*below*), which incorporates the reconstructed seventeenth-century White Horse Inn, made famous by Scott.

The Firth of Forth is spanned by two great bridges. The older, the famous railway bridge, was built at the end of the nineteenth century and opened in 1890. It is over a mile and a half in length and at its highest point is 360 feet above the water. The other bridge is the new Forth Road Bridge (*upper right*), a magnificent suspension bridge with a total length of about 6,000 feet. It provides twin carriage-ways, two footpaths and two cycle tracks and has a minimum clearance above high water of 150 feet. The main cables from which the roadway is suspended are 26 inches in diameter. The new bridge was opened by Her Majesty the Queen in 1964 and replaces the ferry which crossed the river from North to South Queensferry.

Seventeen miles west of Edinburgh is Linlithgow, the county town of West Lothian, and here in the Palace (*lower right*) was born the ill-fated Mary Queen of Scots in 1542. The oldest part of the palace, which was burned down in 1746, is Edward I's tower which dates from the early fourteenth century. Of interest are the Great Hall, the Chapel and the Royal Apartments.

La « Royal Mile » s'étend du Château jusqu'au Palais de Holyrood. Près du Palais se trouve White Horse Close (*ci-contre, à gauche*) avec une ancienne auberge qui date du 17e siècle. Le nouveau pont routier du Forth (*ci-dessus*), qui réunit les deux rives du fleuve, fut ouvert en 1964. Dans le Palais de Linlithgow (*à gauche*) naquit la malheureuse Mary, Reine des Écossais.

Die „Royal Mile" erstreckt sich von der Burg bis zum Palast Holyrood. Neben dem Palast befindet sich White Horse Close (*gegenüber*), wo ein aus dem 17. Jahrhundert stammendes Wirtshaus zu sehen ist. Die neue Brücke über den Firth of Forth (*oben*) wurde 1964 für den Autoverkehr freigegeben. Im Palast von Linlithgow (*links*) wurde 1542 Mary, Königin der Schotten, geboren.

Le Château de Dirleton (*ci-dessus*) fut bâti au 13e siècle. Deux cents ans plus tard on y joignit une maison dans le style Renaissance. Le Château de Thirlestane (*ci-contre*), siège de la famille Maitland, se trouve dans Lauderdale dans le comté de Berwickshire. Sir Walter Scott gît dans l'Abbaye de Dryburgh (*à droite*) qui est située dans la vallée du Tweed.

Das Schloß Dirleton (*oben*) wurde im 13. Jahrhundert erbaut. Zweihundert Jahre später wurde ein Haus im Renaissancestil angebaut. Das Schloß Thirlestane (*gegenüber*), einst Stammhaus der Familie Maitland, befindet sich im Lauderdale in Berwickshire. Sir Walter Scott wurde in der Dryburgh-Abtei (*rechts*) beigesetzt.

From Edinburgh the coastal road to the east extends along the estuary of the Forth to North Berwick. Just short of that royal borough is Dirleton, reputed to be one of the most charming villages in Scotland, which boasts the ruins of a castle dating from the thirteenth century (*upper left*). Additions to the original fortification were made in the fifteenth century and two hundred years later a Renaissance house was joined to it.

Thirlestane Castle (*above*) is in Lauderdale and was the ancestral home of the Maitlands. It was built in the late sixteenth century probably incorporating Lauder Fort which was one of Edward I's Scottish fortifications. The present house dates largely from the seventeenth century and is noted for its fine plasterwork.

Dryburgh has a special niche in Scottish hearts, for in the Abbey (*lower left*) lie buried Sir Walter Scott, his wife and other members of his family, and also Field-Marshal Earl Haig and his wife. The Abbey was founded in the middle of the twelfth century and although of no considerable size it has a most beautiful situation in the valley of the Tweed. In 1544 the Abbey was destroyed by the Earl of Hertford and today there remain only the Chapter House, parts of the West Front and North Transept, and a few other fragments.

« Le panorama de Scott » (*ci-dessus*), en regardant vers les collines d'Eildon en Basse-Écosse. Scott aimait bien cette vue et décrivit dans son poème *The Lay of the Last Minstrel* l'Abbaye de Melrose (*ci-contre, à droite*) qui est située près de sa propre maison à Abbotsford. Les ruines de l'Abbaye de Melrose datent des 14e et 15e siècles. On dit que le cœur de Robert Bruce est enterré dans l'église de l'abbaye. L'Abbaye de Jedburgh (*ci-contre, à gauche*) fut également détruite par les Anglais pendant le 16e siècle, mais les ruines comportent un beau portail et une tour massive romanesques.

Scott liebte die Aussicht auf die Eildonhügel am Tweedufer (*oben*). Nach einer Sage wurden die drei Gipfel binnen einer einzigen Nacht durch Teufelswerk erschaffen. Scott beschrieb in seinem Gedicht „The Lay of the Last Minstrel" die Melroseabtei (*gegenüber, rechts*), deren Ruinen aus den 14. und 15. Jahrhunderten stammen. Das Herz von Robert Bruce, der die Abtei wiedererbaut hatte, soll in der Kirche liegen. Die Jedburgh-Abtei (*gegenüber, links*) wurde, wie die Melroser, im 16. Jahrhundert von den Engländern zerstört. Die Ruine der Abteikirche steht noch.

The rolling hills and pleasant valleys of the Scottish Lowlands present an ever-changing panorama of colour. The eastern part of the Lowlands embraces the Scott country – the district around Galashiels, Selkirk and Montrose – which will always be associated with the novelist and poet. From Bemersyde Hill, near his home at Abbotsford, 'Scotts View' embraces the valley of the Tweed and the Eildon Hills (*upper left*). Of the three summits the middle one is the highest (1,385 feet) and from it Scott claimed he could point out over forty places 'famous in war and verse'. According to legend the three summits were created out of one by a demon in a single night.

The shortest route from Newcastle to Edinburgh crosses the border at Carter Bar, where the last Border skirmish between the Scots and the English took place in 1575. Ten miles further on is Jedburgh, the county town of Roxburghshire, with the imposing ruins of its sandstone Abbey (*lower left*) which dates from the first half of the twelfth century. During the border struggles the Abbey was considerably damaged and finally sacked in 1545. The remains now standing are those of the Abbey church; they include the walls of the nave, the Norman west doorway and the restored Norman tower. Queen Mary's House, where the ill-fated queen recuperated after her arduous journey on horseback to visit the wounded Bothwell in Hermitage Castle, is now a museum.

Melrose Abbey (*below*) was also founded in the twelfth century and, like Jedburgh, suffered from the English invasions, but the ruins are considerable and there are fine examples of intricate stone vaulting. What we see today is largely of fourteenth- and fifteenth-century date and was the eastern part of the Abbey church, the Chapter House and reredorter, and parts of the cloister. It is said that the heart of Robert Bruce rests beneath the East Window. He had restored the abbey in 1326 and bequeathed his heart to it; Douglas was carrying it to the Holy Land when he was attacked by the Moors and Bruce's heart was returned to his native land. Sir Walter Scott, whose description of the Abbey in *The Lay of the Last Minstrel* is well known, had his home at Abbotsford, some two and a half miles to the west. His house, built in 1817 in the popular 'Scottish Baronial' style, is kept as it was in the poet's lifetime.

Dans la vallée du Yarrow dans le Selkirkshire, qui a été l'inspiration de plusieurs poètes, particulièrement Scott et Wordsworth, se trouve le Château de Newark (*ci-dessous, en haut*), ancien pavillon de chasse. Traquair House (*ci-dessous, en bas*), qui date du 17ᵉ siècle, est située près d'Innerleithen dans le comté de Peebles. Le Lac de Sainte Marie (St Mary's Loch) (*ci-contre*) fut décrit par Scott dans *Marmion*.

Im Yarrowtal in der Grafschaft von Selkirk, das viele Dichter inspiriert hat, steht das Newarkschloß (*unten*), ein früheres königliches Jagdhäuschen. Traquair House (*ganz unten*), das aus dem 17. Jahrhundert stammt, befindet sich in der Nähe von Innerleithen in der Grafschaft von Peebles. Der St. Mary's See (*gegenüber*), in einer Talsenke unter den Selkirk-Bergen, wurde von Sir Walter Scott in „Marmion" beschrieben.

The valley of the River Yarrow in Selkirkshire has inspired many poets, notably among them Scott and Wordsworth, to verse in praise of its serene beauty. Nearly four miles from Selkirk we cross the General's Bridge, built by General Mackay, and reach Newark Castle (*upper left*) one of four Scottish castles named 'Newark'. This one is a strongly built royal hunting lodge of the fifteenth century and has the arms of James I on its western wall.

Traquair House (*lower left*) is situated just over a mile to the south of Innerleithen on Quair Water, a tributary of the Tweed. It is a solid-looking seventeenth-century mansion, incorporating an ancient tower, and is certainly one of the oldest inhabited houses in Scotland. The gates to the entrance avenue were closed in 1796 when the seventh Countess of Traquair died, the Earl decreeing that they would never again be opened until another Countess lived at Traquair.

St Mary's Loch (*above*), through which flows the River Yarrow, lies in a depression among the hills of Selkirkshire. It is 'the lone St Mary's silent lake' of Scott's *Marmion*. Near the lake stands a statue of James Hogg, the shepherd-poet of Ettrick who was befriended by Scott. These two, De Quincey, Christopher North, and other successful men of letters used to frequent Tibbie Shiel's Inn, at the head of the loch which is a favourite anglers' resort. Tibbie Shiel, whose real name was Isabella Richardson, lived to be over ninety.

Dumfries was made a royal burgh in the twelfth century when William the Lion was King of Scotland and its oldest charter dates from 1395, but Dumfries owes its more recent fame to Robert Burns who lived here from 1791 until his death in 1796. His house is now a museum where relics, manuscripts and books which belonged to or which are associated with him, are preserved. Burns was first buried in St Michael's Churchyard but in 1815 his body was re-interred in a mausoleum provided by his admirers, and here also rest his wife and his sons. The old stone bridge over the River Nith (*below*) was built in the thirteenth century by Devorguilla, the mother of John de Baliol, the founder of the Oxford college which bears his name. Six of the original arches remain and the bridge is still used by pedestrians. There are three other bridges across the River Nith. Dumfries proper is situated on the east side of the river; on the western bank is Maxwelltown which became incorporated with Dumfries in 1929. The burgh museum in Maxwelltown also contains relics of Robert Burns.

Loch Trool (*upper right*) and Glen Trool in the Galloway uplands now form part of an extensive natural forest park. The loch is about a mile and a half in length and its shores are beautifully wooded; many regard Loch Trool as one of the most attractive places in the whole of Scotland. Five miles to the north rises Merrick (2,764 feet), the highest mountain south of the Clyde, and the whole district abounds in exhilarating walks for the energetic visitor.

Before the regular ferry service between Stranraer and Larne was established in 1849, Portpatrick (*lower right*) was the terminus of the mail steamers to Donagadee in Ireland, from which it is only twenty-one miles away. Indeed legend tells us that St Patrick accomplished the crossing with a single stride! The harbour, which had been built at great expense, has suffered greatly from its exposure to winter storms and is now of little commercial use. A mile to the south-east the ruins of Dunskey Castle, which was built early in the sixteenth century, stand perched on a cliff, looking across the North Channel to the Irish coast.

A Dumfries la Rivière Nith est enjambée par un pont en pierre qui date du 13ᵉ siècle (*ci-contre*). La maison, où le poète Robert Burns passa les dernières années de sa vie, et où il mourut en 1796, est maintenant un musée. Glen Trool et son charmant lac (*ci-dessus*) font partie du Parc National des Forêts de Galloway, province du sud-ouest de l'Écosse. Portpatrick (*à gauche*) fut autrefois un port pour l'Irlande.

Eine Steinbrücke aus dem 13. Jahrhundert überspannt den Nithfluß bei Dumfries (*gegenüber*). Das Haus, wo der Dichter Robert Burns seine letzten Lebensjahre verbrachte und wo er 1796 starb, ist heute ein Museum. Glen Trool und sein See (*oben*) sind ein Teil des Nationalforstes von Galloway, der südwestlichen Provinz Schottlands. Portpatrick (*links*) war einst der Hafen, von dem eine Fähre nach Irland fuhr.

Culzean Castle, œuvre de Robert Adam, possède un escalier finement dessiné (ci-dessus) et renferme les reliques des Kennedy. Girvan (ci-contre, en haut) est une plage populaire et un port consacré à la pêche. De Fairlie, où se dresse un château du 16e siècle, on aperçoit le Firth of Clyde et l'Île d'Arran (à droite).

Culzean Casle (oben) ist der Wohnsitz des Marquis of Ailsa, eines Abkömmlings des Geschlechts der Kennedy. Von Ayr führt die Küstenstrasse nach Girvan (oben rechts), einer kleinen Stadt mit einem reizenden Fischereihafen am Firth of Clyde. Von Fairlie hat man einen grandiosen Blick auf den Firth of Clyde mit der Insel Arran im Hintergrund (rechts).

Culzean Castle, the seat of the Marquis of Ailsa, a descendant of the Kennedy family, is situated on the coast some fourteen miles south-west of Ayr. The present imposing building is the work of Robert Adam, whose finely proportioned staircase (*upper left*) is a notable feature of the interior. The State Rooms contain many relics of the Kennedys, and part of the upper floor was presented to President (then General) Eisenhower as a Scottish home. In 1945 the castle and its grounds were acquired by the National Trust.

The coastal road from Ayr continues to Girvan, a small port with fine views of the Firth of Clyde. Its harbour (*above*) is chiefly devoted to fishing, but the town is popular as a holiday resort, with excellent bathing and a well-known golf course. A popular sea trip is to Ailsa Crag, ten miles off the coast, which is a haunt of many sea birds and a notable landmark for mariners, to whom it is known as Paddy's Milestone, as it is approximately half-way between Glasgow and Belfast. The rock rises directly from the sea to a height of over 1,000 feet.

From Fairlie, just to the south of Largs, there is a fine view of the Firth of Clyde with the island of Arran in the distance (*lower left*). Fairlie, which has the ruins of a sixteenth-century castle, is a prosperous seaside resort and is also well-known as a yacht-building centre.

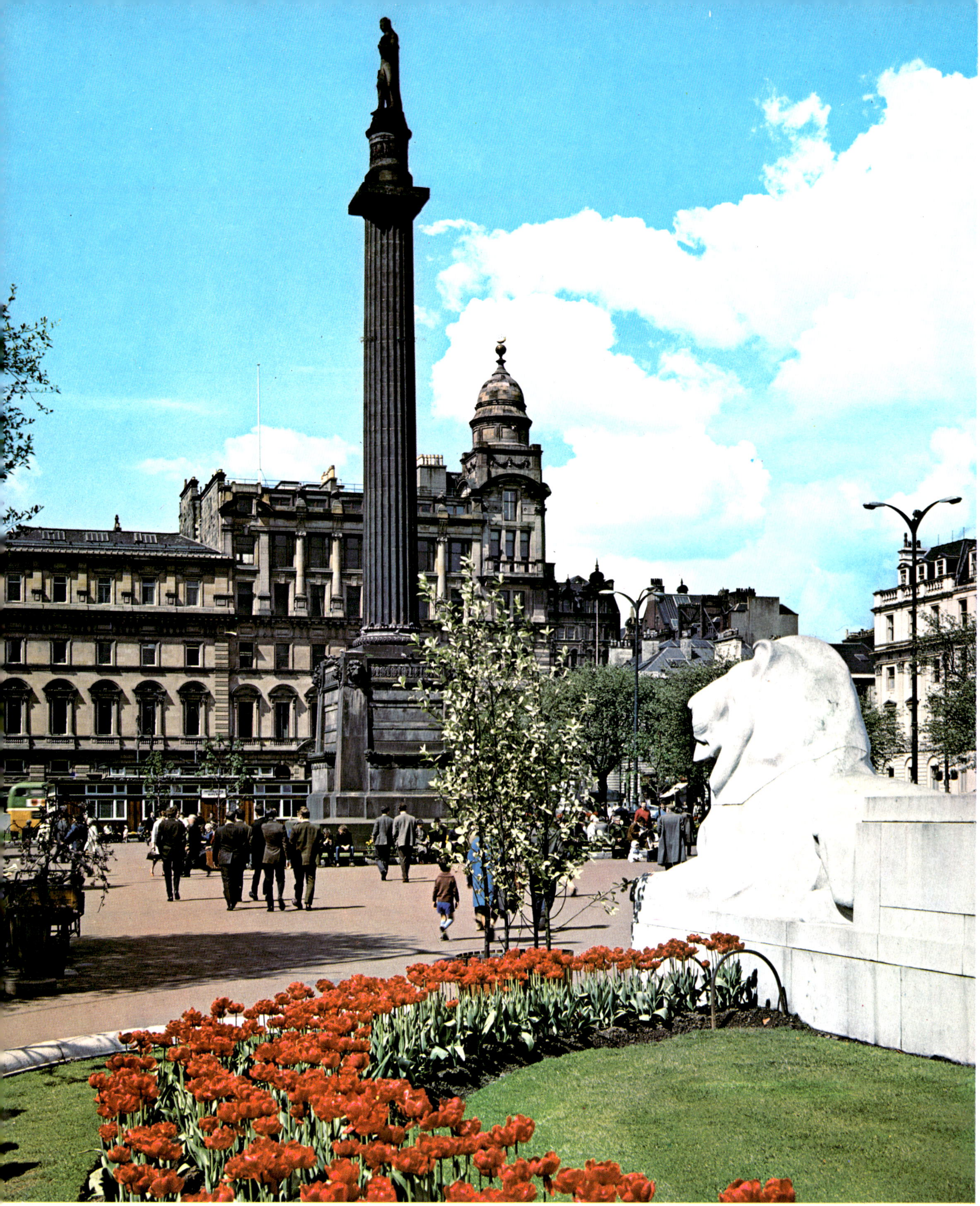

Glasgow grew up in the eighteenth century, when industry and commerce began to convert the town, described by Defoe as 'the most beautiful little city in Europe', into the huge sprawling metropolis and seaport of the twentieth century. Yet Glasgow still has its links with the past, especially its beautiful twelfth-century Cathedral on the site of the grave of St Kentigen, or as he is better known, St Mungo. The centre of the city is George Square (*left*) where stand the City Chambers, built last century in the style of the Italian Renaissance. In front of them rises an eighty-foot-high column surmounted by a statue of Sir Walter Scott. Glasgow University is the second oldest in Scotland; it has a fine situation overlooking Kelvingrove Park (*below left*), through which the River Kelvin flows to the Clyde. The University was founded in 1451, but the present buildings, which were designed by Sir Gilbert Scott, date from 1870. As a shipbuilding centre and seaport Glasgow is famous throughout the world. Britain's largest passenger liners and many of her finest naval ships have been built here, and the city has over fourteen miles of docks and excellent facilities for the handling of cargoes.

Glasgow is an excellent tourist centre, and there are a great many famous and beautiful places which can be visited in a day. Undoubtedly the most popular recreation is a sail down the Clyde in one of the busy little ships which link Glasgow with most of the resorts of the Clyde estuary. However, if the visitor leaves the river and ventures inland he will find some delightful spots such as the valley of the River Cart (*below right*) in Renfrewshire. The Cart – there are actually two streams, the White and the Black Cart – enters the Clyde opposite Clydebank, the busy shipbuilding part of Glasgow.

Au milieu de Georges Square, Glasgow (*ci-contre*) s'élève la colonne de Sir Walter Scott. L'université, fondée en 1451, donne sur Kelvingrove Park (*ci-dessous, à gauche*). Glasgow est connu pour ses chantiers navals, ses 22 km. de quais, mais aussi pour la Clyde et ses vallées. Pas loin de la cité se trouve la charmante vallée de la Cart (*ci-dessous à droite*).

Den Mittelpunkt von Glasgow bildet der Georgsplatz (*gegenüber*), mit dem Rathaus, eidem Bau aus dem letzten Jahrhundert. Von der Universität Glasgow hat man einen schönen Blick auf den Kelvingrove Park (*unten links*). Auch die Umgebung der Stadt ist reich an landschaftlichen Schönheiten. Unweit der Großstadt befindet sich das schöne Tal der Cart (*unten rechts*).

Dollar, in Clackmannanshire, is famous for its academy, founded by John MacNab, a native of the town who made his fortune at sea. The original building, for which the architect was Sir William Playfair, was erected in 1819, and considerable additions were made during the next ninety years. No less famous is Castle Campbell (*below*) to the north of the town, which was built in the fifteenth century on a hill between the Burn of Care and the Burn of Sorrow. Small wonder that it was once known as the Castle of Gloom. John Knox is known to have preached here before his journey to Geneva.

Stirling is the principal gateway to the Highlands and as such has held an eventful history. The town is dominated by its castle (*upper right*), crowning a 300-foot-high bluff which played a major role during the struggle for Scottish independence. In 1297 William Wallace captured the castle from the English at the Battle of Stirling Bridge, and it was to raise the siege of the castle that Edward II fought the Battle of Bannockburn. In spite of the king's superior forces he was, however, defeated by Robert the Bruce, and Bannockburn ranks as a model of military tactics of the time. Both Mary Queen of Scots and her son James VI were crowned at Stirling, which today is a thriving town with woollen and leather manufactures.

Five miles south-west of Kinross, Aldie Castle (*lower right*) stands perched on a hill looking towards the Cleish Hills. It was an ancient seat of the Mercers of Aldie. Kinross itself is on Loch Leven, famous for its fishing and for the castle where Mary Queen of Scots was imprisoned for nearly a year before making her escape with the aid of William Douglas, a lad of eighteen.

L'académie de Dollar fut fondée en 1819 par John MacNab. Castle Campbell (*ci-contre*) fut construit au 15e siècle à Dollar. Mary, reine des Écossais, et son fils, James VI, furent couronnés à Stirling, dont le château (*ci-dessus, en haut*) fut conquis par William Wallace en 1297. Aldie Castle (*ci-dessus, en bas*) est situé près de Kinross.

Aus dem 15. Jahrhundert stammt das berühmte Schloß Campbell (*genenüber*). John Knox predigte hier, bevor er nach Genf zog. Stirling, bedeutend in der wechselvollen Geschichte Schottlands, wird beherrscht von seinem Schloß (*ganz oben*) auf einem Steilabhang. Von Schloß Aldie (*oben*) hat man einen weiten Ausblick bis zu den Cleish Hills.

The county of Fife, often still called the Kingdom of Fife, lies between the estuaries of the Forth and the Tay, forming a peninsula with the sea on its eastern flank. The coast is particularly attractive and is sometimes referred to as the 'Scottish Riviera'. Crail, one of the oldest of the royal burghs of Fife, is some four miles north-east of Anstruther. Traces remain of a nunnery and of the royal hunting lodge which once stood here. The little harbour (*below*), now only used by fishing boats, was at one time a flourishing seaport.

Anstruther (*upper right*) is really three places in one – the royal burghs of Kilrenny, Anstruther Easter and Anstruther Wester. Here the eminent Scottish theologian Dr Thomas Chalmers was born. In the churchyard of Anstruther Wester there was discovered an ancient lidless coffin which, it was claimed, was that of St Adrian. The coffin was supposed to have floated here from the chapel on the Isle of May in the Firth of Forth. Anstruther is a thriving fishing port and has a famous annual fair. Of great interest is The Manse, which dates from the end of the sixteenth century and is reputed to be the oldest inhabited manse in the whole of Scotland.

St Andrews is famous on three counts: it has the most important golf club – the Royal and Ancient – in the world, it has the oldest university in Scotland, and its Cathedral, now only a ruin, was the largest in the country. The Cathedral (*lower right*), the remains of which are beautifully preserved, was completed early in the twelfth century; the tower and choir of St Rule's Church are still standing within the Cathedral precincts. St Andrews University which now includes the University of Dundee, was founded in 1412; one of its treasures is the pulpit from which Knox preached in the Town Church.

Le comté de Fife s'étend entre la Forth et la Tay. A Crail, près d'Anstruther, subsistent les restes d'un couvent et du pavillon royal de chassè. Le petit port (*ci-contre, à gauche*) fut autrefois un important port de mer. Anstruther (*ci-dessus*) vit naître le théologien Thomas Chalmers. St Andrews possède le plus important golf club du monde, l'université la plus vieille d'Écosse, fondée en 1412, et la cathédrale (*gauche*) qui fut la plus grande d'Écosse.

Crail ist eine der ältesten Städte in der Grafschaft Fife. Sein einst wichtiger Hochseehafen beherbergt heute nur noch einige Fischerboote (*ganz links*). In Anstruther (*oben*) wurde der große Theologe, Dr. Thomas Chalmers, geboren. St. Andrews ist berühmt wegen dreier Dinge: sein Golfklub ist der bedeutendste in der Welt, die dortige Universität ist die älteste in Schottland, und die Kathedrale, heute nur noch eine Ruine (*links*), war einst die größte im ganzen Land.

The River Tay, which rises in the Grampians and enters the North Sea by a tidal estuary twenty-five miles long, has a serene beauty of its own, especially in its lower reaches. The photograph above is of the Tay valley from Kinnoull Hill to the east of Perth. The ruined tower on the summit belongs to Kinfauns Castle, a nineteenth-century Gothic edifice, designed by Sir Robert Smirke who also built the Royal Mint and the British Museum.

On the south bank of the Tay are the ruins of Elcho Castle (*upper right*), the ancestral seat of the Earls of Wymss. It is one of the most complete examples remaining of the fortified houses of the sixteenth century. The house, which was constructed from materials from a near-by quarry, is notable for the turrets projecting from the upper floors and for the wrought-iron grilles protecting the windows.

The Fair City of Perth, the capital of Scotland until the middle of the fifteenth century, has had a long and eventful history, from the foundation of the earliest monasteries until the Jacobite risings in the eighteenth century. The town has a fine situation on the right bank of the Tay (*lower right*) between two open spaces called 'Inches'. The former name of Perth was St Johnstoun, recalling that the Church of St John played a prominent role in the fortunes of the city. Forty altars were once to be found in this old church, where in 1559 John Knox preached the sermon which incited his followers 'to purge the churches of idolatry'.

La Tay prend sa source dans les Grampians et se jette dans la Mer du Nord par un estuaire de 32 km. La photographie ci-contre est prise de Kinnoull Hill, à l'est de Perth. La tour en ruines appartient au Kinfauns Castle (19ᵉ siècle). Sur la rive sud de la Tay se dressent les ruines d'Elcho Castle (*ci-dessous, en haut*), datant du 16ᵉ siècle. Perth, capitale de l'Écosse jusqu'au milieu du 15ᵉ siècle, s'étend sur la rive droite de la Tay (*ci-dessous, en bas*), entre deux espaces appelés « Inches ».

Die linksstehende Aufnahme zeigt das Flußtal des Tay von Kinnoull Hill bis östlich von Perth. Der Unterlauf dieses Flusses ist besonders reizvoll. Am Südufer des Tay stehen die Ruinen des Schlosses Elcho (*unten*), seit Urzeiten Ahnensitz der Herzöge von Wymss. Bis in die Mitte des 15. Jahrhunderts war Perth die Hauptstadt Schottlands, herrlich gelegen am rechten Flußufer des Tay (*ganz unten*). Der ursprüngliche Name der Stadt war St. Johnstoun.

Glamis Castle (*above*) is situated near the village of the same name, about five miles from Forfar. Readers of Shakespeare will be familiar with its associations with *Macbeth*, and the castle is certainly an ancient foundation. The present building dates from the seventeenth century, but it was partially rebuilt in 1800 after a fire. Both the Old and the Young Pretenders used the castle as their headquarters. In 1930 Princess Margaret was born at Glamis Castle; her mother, then the Duchess of York, was the daughter of the Earl of Strathmore, the owner of the castle. Glamis Castle, which is open to the public in the summer, has a fine collection of armour, tapestries and pictures. There is a most interesting collection of old domestic and agricultural exhibits in the Angus Folk Museum in Glamis village.

Glen Clova bites deep into the Grampians from Kirremuir, ascending the valley of the River South Esk. Milton of Clova (*upper right*), an isolated village some six miles along the valley, is a favourite resort of anglers and a good starting-point for long walks towards Deeside. Overlooking the village are the scanty remains of Clova Castle, where Charles II came, hoping to enlist the help of the Highlanders during his trouble with the Presbyterians. The road along Glen Clova ends at Braedownie but good walkers can reach Braemar by taking the path via 'Jock's Road' and Glen Callater.

Glen Esk, the valley of the North Esk, strikes into the Grampians north of Brechin, where the twelfth-century Cathedral was well restored in 1901. The Cathedral, which is now used as the parish church, is notable for its tall round tower, probably a century older than the rest of the building. Some fifteen miles along Glen Esk, near the end of the road, stand the ruins of Invermark Castle (*lower right*), a former residence of the Stirling clan which was used as a strongpoint in the days of the struggles against the Highlanders. Beyond Invermark Castle a track leads to lonely Loch Lee.

Glamis Castle (*ci-contre, à gauche*), à 8 km. de Forfar, date du 17ᵉ siècle. La Princesse Margaret y naquit en 1930. Milton of Clova (*à gauche*) est un village isolé dominé par Clova Castle, maintenant en ruines. Dans le Glen Esk se dressent les ruines d'Invermark Castle (*ci-dessous*), ancienne résidence du clan Stirling.

Die Burg Glamis (*ganz links*) in der Nähe eines gleichnamigen Ortes wird Shakespeare-Kenner sogleich an Macbeth erinnern; tatsächlich ist diese Burg uralt. Milton of Clova (*links*), ein abgelegener Ort im Clova-Tal, ist ein guter Ausgangspunkt für lange Wanderungen in Richtung Deeside. Tief im Inneren des Esk-Tales befindet sich die Ruine des Schlosses Invermark (*unten*), früher der Sitz des Stirling-Klans.

Stonehaven, the county town of Kincardineshire, lies some fourteen miles south-west of Aberdeen and it is a favourite resort of Aberdonians. Its picturesque harbour (*below*), flanked by the mouths of the Carron and Cowie rivers, stamps it as a fishing port; on the north pier stands an old storehouse which became a tollbooth in the seventeenth century. The town enjoys an invigorating climate and excellent amenities. The cliff scenery and caves in the vicinity are particularly attractive. A mile and a half to the south Dunnottar Castle (*lower right*) perches on a huge rock with the sea on three sides and a deep chasm on the other. The ruins of this fortress are probably of fourteenth-century date, but there was a castle here which was captured and burned by Wallace in 1297. During the Commonwealth the Scottish regalia was kept in the Castle, and, being in some danger of capture, was smuggled out to safety by the wife of the minister of Kinneff who was visiting the Governor's wife. Until the Restoration the regalia lay hidden beneath the floor of Kinneff Church.

Now owned by the Scottish National Trust, Crathes Castle (*upper right*) was begun about the middle of the sixteenth century. It stands near Banchory to the north of the River Dee and is a fine example of that style of domestic architecture which is usually called 'Scottish Baronial'. Skilful restoration in the last century uncovered painted ceilings of Jacobean date which are held to be the best in the country. The most precious possession of Crathes, which was the home of the Burnett family for over six hundred years, is the ivory 'Horn of Leys', associated with Robert the Bruce. The gardens, which were laid out in the eighteenth century, are notable for their mighty hedges of Irish yew and unusual shrubs.

Stonehaven, capitale du Kincardineshire, possède un port pittoresque entre la Carron et la Courie (*à gauche*). Au sud Dunnottar Castle (*ci-dessus, en bas*) se dresse sur un roc, face à la mer. Il date probablement du 14e siècle. Crathes Castle (*ci-dessus, en haut*), commencé vers 1550, reflète le style « Scottish Baronial ».

Stonehaven in der Grafschaft Kincardineshire besitzt einen malerischen Fischereihafen mit einem alten Zollgebäude aus dem 17. Jahrhundert (*links*). Knapp zwei km. im Süden thront Schloß Dunnottar auf einem gewaltigen Felsen (*oben*). Crathes Schloß (*ganz oben*) stammt aus der Mitte des 16. Jahrhunderts.

Aberdeen, the 'Granite City', is Scotland's third largest burgh. Built chiefly of granite, the town has varied industries and is popular as a holiday resort. The beaches are sandy and there is a fine promenade two miles in length. Fishing has long been of importance to Aberdeen, and the harbour (*below*) is often thronged with vessels. Two rivers, the Dee and the Don, flank the city, whose Cathedral, dedicated to St Machar, was founded in 1136. Aberdeen has a distinguished university, and is an excellent centre from which to explore Eastern Scotland. The River Dee rises in the Cairngorms and flows in a generally easterly direction to enter the sea at Aberdeen. For 65 miles of its course it is accessible by road, the valley becoming progressively more beautiful as one travels upstream.

The coastal lowland extends north-east from Aberdeen to Fraserburgh and then westwards to the Moray Firth through the counties of Banff, Moray and Nairn, the coasts of which are, like Aberdeen, studded with fishing ports. At Dufftown in Banffshire are the ruins of Balvenie Castle (*lower right*). It is reputed to have been the home of the notorious Wolf of Badenoch but was later owned by the Atholl family whose family motto appears on the front. The curtain wall is probably of earlier date than the rest of the Castle, the remains of which date principally from the fifteenth and sixteenth centuries. As it stands today it is one of the largest castles of the northern counties.

Elgin Cathedral (*upper right*) was once called the 'Lantern of the North' and was undoubtedly one of the finest of Scottish Cathedrals. It was founded early in the thirteenth century but in 1390 was burned by the Wolf of Badenoch. In 1506 the central tower collapsed, and although strenuous efforts were made to repair the damage, during the troubled period following the Reformation the Cathedral was allowed to decay. Fortunately, the ruins, which include the West Front and the Chapter House, are now in the care of the Ministry of Works.

Aberdeen est un port de pêche actif (*ci-dessus*). La cathédrale fut bâtie en 1136. Balvenie Castle (*ci-contre, en bas*) est l'un des plus grands d'Écosse. Elgin Cathedral (*ci-contre, en haut*) fut construite au 18e siècle.

Aberdeen ist die drittgrößte Stadt Schottlands mit einem bedeutenden Fischereihafen (*oben*). Schloß Balvenie (*rechts*) stammt aus dem 16. Jahrhundert. Die Kathedrale von Elgin (*rechts oben*) war eine der schönsten Schottlands.

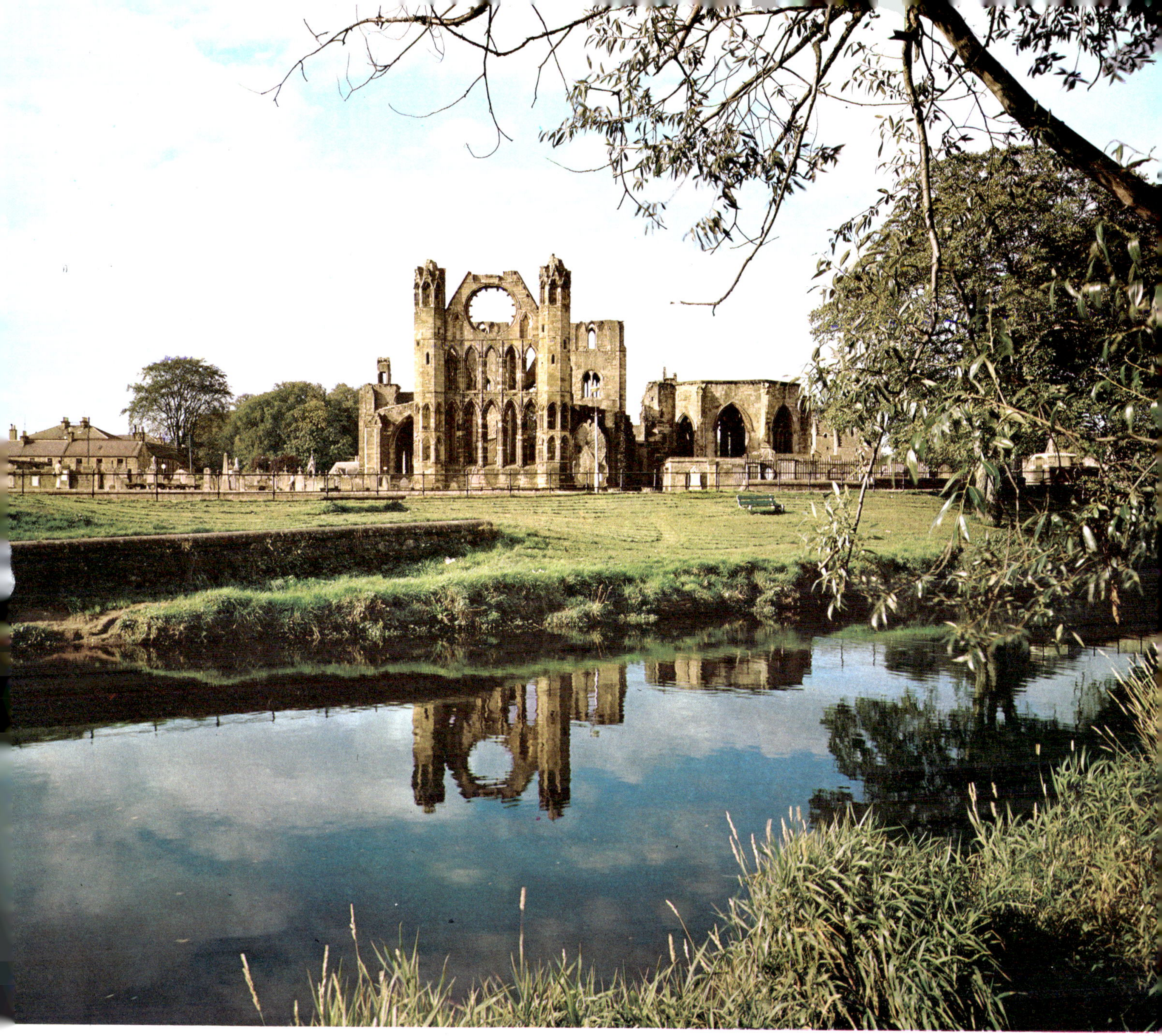

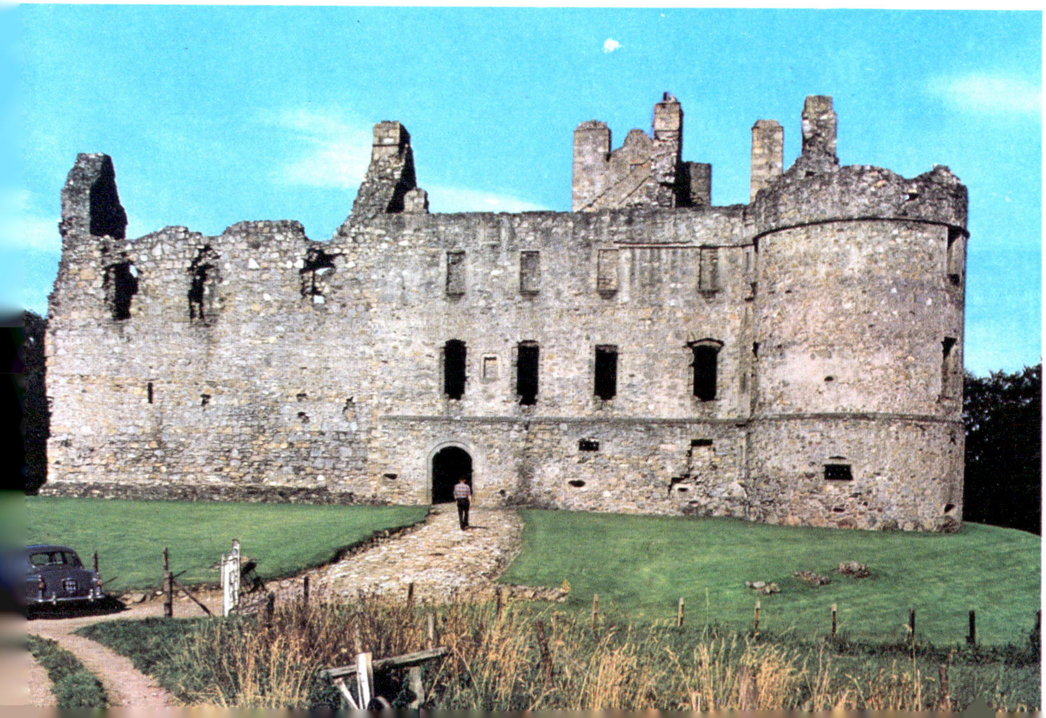

The Highlands

The Scottish Highlands, a region of majestic mountains, beautiful river valleys, freshwater lochs and sea-lochs, contain some of the grandest scenery in the British Isles. They lie north and west of a line joining the mouth of the Clyde with Stonehaven, excluding the low-lying region of the east coast and the islands of Orkney and Shetland. The mountains of the Highlands, composed of igneous rocks, reach their greatest altitude in the Grampian range to the east of Fort William, with Ben Nevis (4,406 feet) the highest peak in the British Isles. Perhaps the most striking feature of the Scottish Highlands is the profusion of lochs. The sea-lochs are really fiord-like inlets, some of them very long and many very beautiful. Some of the freshwater lochs are less generally accessible, but many have the most romantic of settings, and Loch Lomond is world famous.

When Scotland was a separate kingdom the Highland chieftains ruled their own lands with scant deference to the crown and frequently quarrelled among themselves. But the English were the common enemy and the Highlanders bravely resisted the attempts of Edward I to subjugate them and succeeded in routing the English at Bannockburn. However, in spite of union with the English Crown in 1603 and with the English Parliament in 1707, the Highlanders continued to assert their independence, leading to the Jacobite rebellions of 1715 and 1745 culminating in the defeat at Culloden. The 'Clearances' of the eighteenth and nineteenth centuries further weakened the influence of the Highland clans. Today the picture has changed; tourism has become a major industry and hydro-electric schemes and afforestation are helping to effect something of a recovery in the economic life of the region.

Geographically the Highlands are divided into eastern and western parts by the Great Glen, the valley of Lochs Lochy, Oich and Ness. These three lochs provided nearly forty miles of the waterway known as the Caledonian Canal which Thomas Telford built in the early years of the last century. There are twenty-nine locks on the twenty-one miles of artificial waterway linking the lochs. The canal provides a short cut for ships from the Atlantic to the North Sea. During its early life it was very busy but today it is little used.

Five counties – Caithness, Sutherland, Ross and Cromarty, Inverness and Argyll – lie wholly within the area of the Highlands, together with parts of Dunbarton, Perth, Aberdeen and Banff. Caithness, however, exhibits few of the Highland characteristics; not many of its people are Gaelic-speaking and only in the south of the county does the terrain approach 2,000 feet in height. Norse influence is seen in many of the place-names. Sutherland, on the other hand, is a bleak and mountainous county with few main roads and many lochs. The county suffered greatly during the 'Clearances' of last century, when thousands of the population were forced to move to more prosperous areas, but in recent years efforts have been made to improve the lot of the inhabitants, most of whom are engaged on sheep farming and the production of tweed.

Inverness-shire, Scotland's largest county, is also its most mountainous, and includes within its boundaries part of the Inner and all the Outer Hebrides with the exception of

Lewis which forms part of Ross and Cromarty. The land is mostly unsuitable for arable farming and the principal rural occupations are the rearing of sheep and cattle. Ross and Cromarty extends from the Moray Firth to the Atlantic, and apart from its eastern fringes is a county of moorland and mountain. The finest scenery is found among the sea-lochs of the west coast. Argyllshire, the most southerly of the Highland counties, embraces many of the smaller islands of the Inner Hebrides. Within its borders some of the finest scenery in Scotland is to be found. Crofting is the principal occupation apart from the ever-increasing growth of the tourist industry.

There are three main roads into the Highlands. One, the A9 from Perth, which is the route also followed by the railway, ascends the valley of the Tay and crosses the Grampians to Inverness. Another keeps to the line of the Great Glen, following the eastern shores of Loch Linnhe and Loch Lochy and the western shore of Loch Ness. Braemar and Balmoral can be reached from Aberdeen or Stonehaven, but the fine road from Blairgowrie along Glen Shee and Glen Clunie traverses a magnificent mountain landscape. From Spean Bridge, where there is a noble memorial to the Commandos who trained in the Highlands during the last war, there is a good road across the mountains to Kingussie.

It is the Highlands of Scotland which are the last strongholds of the Gaelic tongue, one of the two main branches of the Celtic language, and nowhere else in the British Isles are family ties more firmly established. Everyone admires the colourful tartans denoting membership of a Scottish clan, and such famous clans as the Campbells, the Macdonalds and the Camerons have their roots in the Highlands. The name 'clan' was originally applied to a group claiming common ancestry who lived as a family on their own lands and served their chief with unbounded loyalty. Although the members of clans may now be widely dispersed, they nevertheless proudly wear the tartan on festive occasions, such as the Highland Games which are held at several centres each year. Events such as 'tossing the caber' are rarely seen elsewhere, but Highland dancing is so popular that it has spread southwards and is now practised and enjoyed in the Lowlands and even in England. It is, however, undoubtedly the skirl of the pipes which makes the most lasting impression on the visitor. To the Highlander this is the symbol of his homeland, the sound which epitomises the spirit of the clan and awakens his Scottish pride.

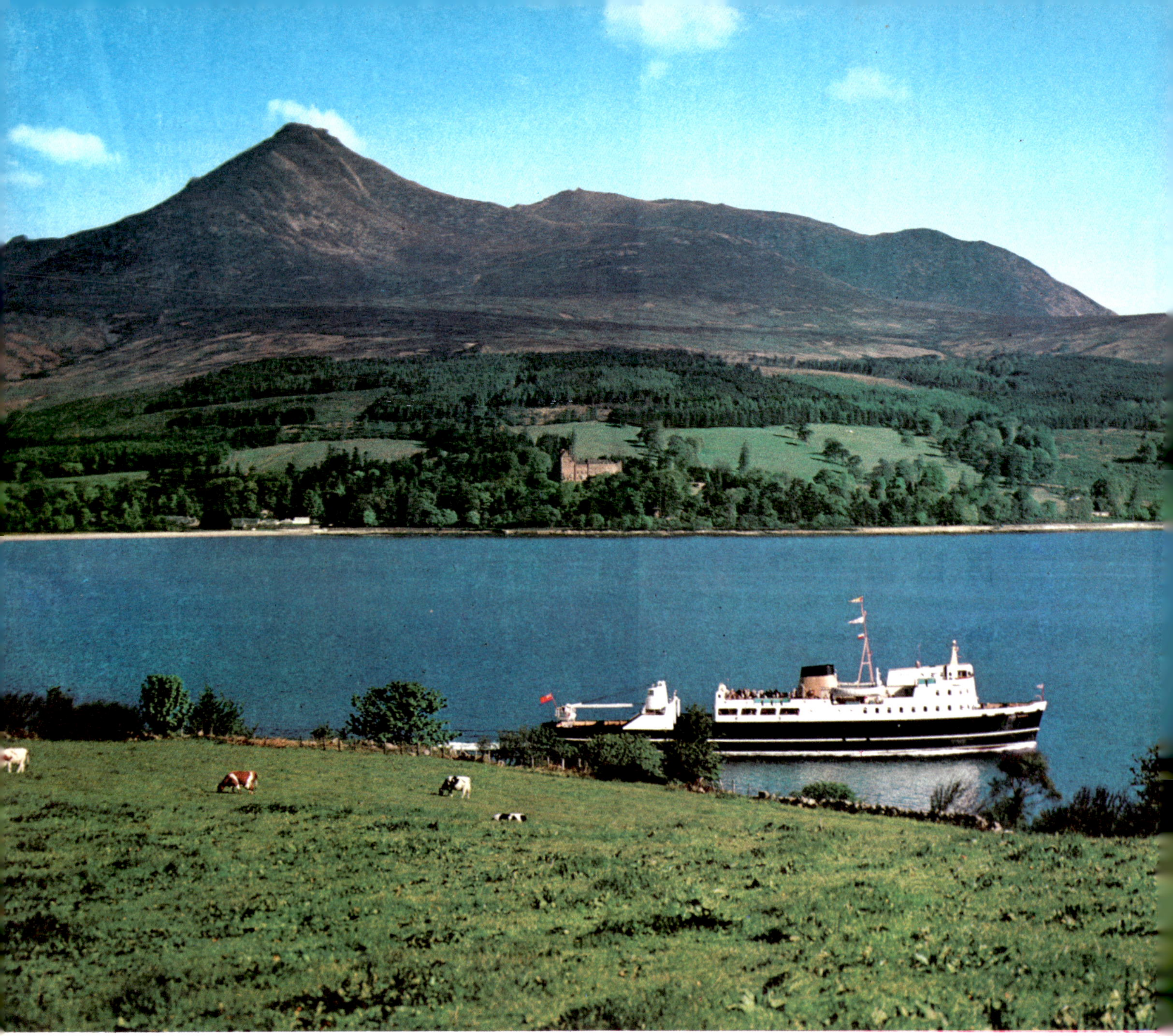

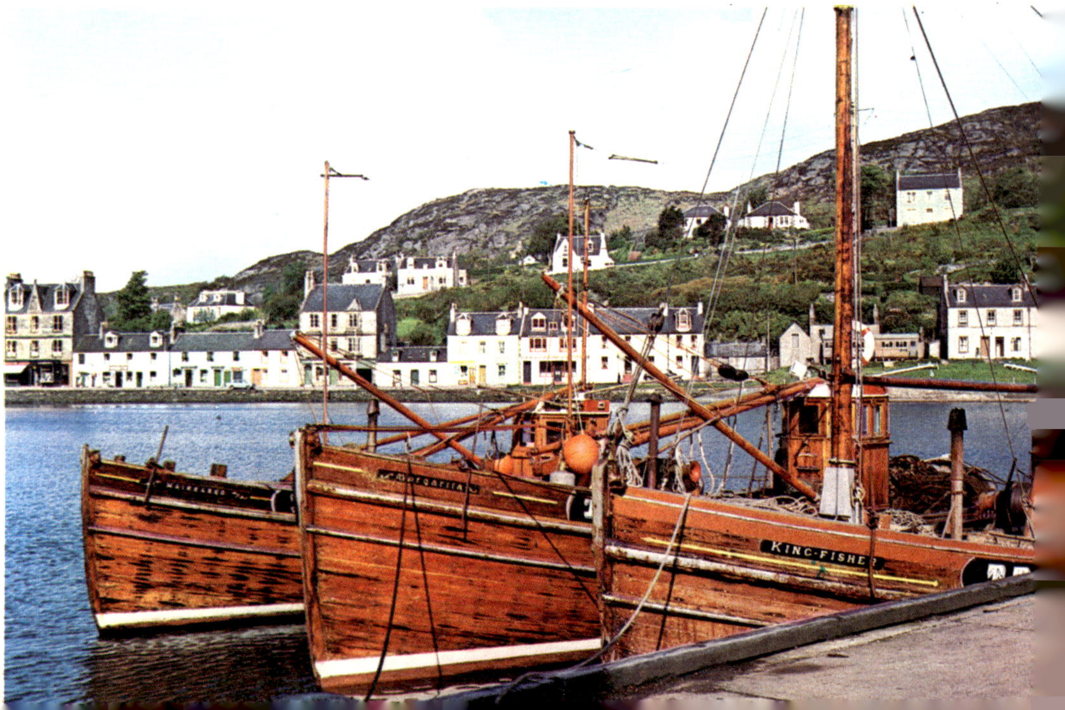
KING-FISHER

The visitor to Glasgow or any of the Clydeside resorts will be well repaid by a trip by boat to the Isle of Arran, the largest of the islands in the Firth of Clyde. Arran is a mountainous island, the highest point being Goat Fell (2,866 feet) seen (*upper left*), with Brodick Castle on the far side of the bay. Brodick Castle has had a chequered history, the earliest building on the site having been sacked by Viking invaders. The present Castle is very largely of eighteenth-century date and it is distinguished in having its own little harbour which was specially constructed for a visit paid by King Edward VII. Since the only means of communication with the mainland is by boat, Arran has remained largely unspoiled, and for this reason is a paradise for those who delight in walking.

Cradling the northern part of the Island of Bute, a favourite holiday resort, the romantic Kyles of Bute (*below*) provide a most delightful day's sailing. Each day in summer one of the Clyde steamers leaves Gourock and sails around the Kyles to Tarbert (*lower left*) and Ardrishaig at the entrance to the Crinan Canal. Many a visitor will be tempted to tarry awhile at Rothesay, the 'capital' of Bute and a particularly attractive holiday resort. On the other side of the island is Tighnabruaich, an equally charming place for a peaceful stay. Leaving the Kyles the ship enters Loch Fyne, the longest sea-loch in the Firth of Clyde and famous for its herring, and calls at Tarbert on the narrow isthmus between East and West Lochs Tarbert. The former is a short inlet facing Loch Fyne, but the West Loch extends south-westwards for ten miles to the Atlantic, and from Tarbert there is a service of steamers to Islay, Jura and the smaller islands of the southern Inner Hebrides. Tarbert boasts a ruined fourteenth-century Castle, once the home of Robert the Bruce.

Goat Fell (755 m.) (*ci-contre, en haut*) est le sommet le plus haut de l'Île d'Arran. Tarbert (*ci-contre, en bas*) est situé sur une presqu'île du Loch Fyne. Les Kyles of Bute (*ci-dessus*) encerclent l'Île de Bute.

Goat Fell (755 m) (*gegenüber, oben*) ist der höchste Gipfel der Insel Arran. Tarbert (*gegenüber, unten*) liegt auf einer Halbinsel am Loch Fyne. Die Kyles of Bute (*oben*) umgeben die Insel Bute.

The Crinan Canal, seen (*above*) at Crinan in Argyllshire, was begun at the end of the eighteenth century and completed in 1817. Its construction enabled small craft to sail from Loch Gulp to the west coast without having to make the long and sometimes dangerous passage around Kintyre. It is nine miles in length and has no fewer than fifteen locks, but today it is used only by pleasure craft. In 1847 Queen Victoria passed through it on her way to Oban.

Loch Fyne is a sea loch which extends deep into the heart of Argyllshire. Near its head is Inveraray, a tourist centre of great charm; its picturesque Castle, built in the Gothic style, is the seat of the Duke of Argyll. In the town is a Celtic cross which came from the monastery founded on Iona in the seventh century. To the north of Inveraray, Dunderave Castle (*upper right*) stands on the shore of the lake. It is the 'Doom Castle' of the novel by Neil Munro.

To the west of Loch Lomond, and separated from it by only a narrow neck of land lies Loch Long. The village of Arrochar (*lower right*) is situated at the head of the loch, behind which rises the peak of Ben Lomond on the further side of Loch Lomond. Arrochar is a favourite starting-point for climbing Ben Arthur, popularly called 'The Cobbler'. From Arrochar the main road to Inveraray ascends the Pass of Glen Croe, over 'Rest and be Thankful' and descends Glen Kinglas.

Le Crinan Canal (*ci-contre*) fut achevé en 1817; il est long de 14 km. et a quinze écluses. Il évite le passage difficile autour de Kintyre, mais aujourd'hui il est peu utilisé. Le Château de Dunderave (*ci-dessous, en haut*) est situé sur la rive du Loch Fyne au nord d'Inveraray. Sur une langue de terre entre le Loch Lomond et le Loch Long se trouve Arrochar (*ci-dessous, en bas*). Derrière le village s'élève Ben Lomond.

Der Crinankanal (*gegenüber*) wurde 1817 vollendet; er vermeidet die lange Seefahrt um Kintyre, wird aber heutzutage wenig benutzt. Er ist 14 km lang und hat 15 Schleusen. Das Schloß Dunderave (*unten*) steht am Ufer des Loch Fyne nördlich von Inveraray. Auf einer Landenge zwischen dem Loch Lomond und dem Loch Long befindet sich Arrochar (*ganz unten*). Hinter dem Dorf ragt der Gipfel von Ben Lomond empor.

Loch Awe in Argyllshire is over twenty miles in length but only about a mile in width except at its northern end. Unlike other long lochs in the Highlands it has no outlet to the sea at the southern point, but drains, in fact, through the Pass of Brander into Loch Etive. There are several islands in the loch, on some of which are the remains of former fortifications, for Loch Awe is in the heart of Campbell country and was in itself a natural moat to their territories in the days of clan warfare. On a rocky spur near the head of the loch stands Kilchurn Castle (*below*), overlooked by the peaks of Ben Cruachan. It was built by Sir Colin Campbell in the fifteenth century and added to in the following two hundred years.

Oban (*upper right*), often called 'the gateway to the Western Highlands', has a fine position on a semicircular bay, sheltered by the island of Kerrera. The town has virtually no traditions for it developed as a resort only during the nineteenth century, but it provides the holidaymaker with a great many opportunities for excursions by road and sea. The view from Pulpit Hill is famous, and behind the town stands McCaig's Folly, intended by its builder to be a museum and art gallery. It provided welcome work for the unemployed of 1897 but McCaig died before it could be completed. Oban harbour is always busy, especially in summer when steamer excursions of a considerable variety attract thousands of visitors, and the port has a great reputation as a yachting centre.

Loch Etive (*lower right*), a sea-loch of about twenty miles in length, stretches from the Glen of Etive to reach the sea at the Firth of Lorne. The head of the loch is accessible by a secondary road from Glencoe which branches off near Kingshouse Hotel. At Connel Ferry Loch Etive is crossed by a bridge carrying the railway from Oban to Ballachulish and a toll carriageway for vehicles. Before the bridge was constructed in 1903, the narrow and dangerous strait was crossed by a ferry.

Le Château de Kilchurn (*ci-contre*), qui date du 15ᵉ siècle, se trouve sur la rive du Loch Awe, à l'ombre de Ben Cruachan. Oban (*ci-dessus*), chef-lieu des Highlands occidentaux, est bien connue des touristes. C'est une ville prospère qui jouit d'une belle situation maritime. Le Loch Étive (*à gauche*) s'étend du Glen Étive jusqu'à l'estuaire de Lorne, sur une distance d'une trentaine de kilomètres.

Das Schloß Kilchurn (*gegenüber*), das aus dem 15. Jahrhundert stammt, steht am Ufer des Loch Awe im Schatten von Ben Cruachan. Jeder Tourist kennt Oban (*oben*), das „Tor zum westlichen Hochland". Es ist sowohl Fischereihafen als auch Vergnügungsort. Der Etivesee (*links*) streckt sich vom Etivetal bis zur Lornemündung. Eine Nebenstrasse führt von Glencoe zum oberen Teil des Sees.

Loch Leven, a fiord-like inlet of Loch Linnhe, lies on the boundary between Argyllshire and Inverness-shire. From the northern shore there is a fine view of the Pap of Glencoe (*above*), standing sentinel above the famous Pass of Glencoe (*upper right*) where the Macdonalds were massacred by the Campbells in 1692. Apart from its historical connections, the pass is one of the most romantic spots in the Highlands in a wildly beautiful setting among the Lorne Mountains. A fine modern road now traverses Glencoe at a lower level than the old one. It is usual to include the whole valley between Rannoch Moor and Loch Leven in the name Glencoe, although the glen proper is the western part of some five miles. Not far below the col is a rocky spur called 'The Study', from which fine views are to be enjoyed. To the north of Loch Leven rise the Mamore Hills (*lower right*) between the loch and Glen Nevis, with Binnein Mor, the highest peak, reaching 3,700 feet. The twin peaks of Ben Vair overlook Ballachulish, a village famous for its slate quarries, from which a car-ferry crosses to North Ballachulish, avoiding a detour round Loch Leven, at the head of which is Kinlochleven, a thriving industrial town with aluminium works powered by water from the Blackwater Reservoir in the hills above. On the island of St Munda in the loch are buried some of those who were slain in the infamous massacre of 1692.

De la rive nord du Loch Leven s'étend une belle perspective des montagnes, dont le Pap of Glencoe domine la scène (*ci-dessus, à gauche*). En 1692 dans le fameux défilé de Glencoe (*ci-dessus*) le Clan Macdonald fut massacré par les Campbell. Au nord du Loch Leven s'élèvent les collines de la Forêt de Mamore (*à gauche*).

Von dem nördlichen Ufer des Loch Leven hat man einen schönen Blick auf den Pap of Glencoe (*oben, links*). Das Glencoejoch (*oben*) ist eine der romantischen Gegenden des Hochlands. Hier wurde der Klan Macdonald von den Campbells im Jahre 1692 niedergemetzelt. Nördlich des Sees ragen die Berge des Mamorwaldes empor (*links*).

Perhaps it is its proximity to Glasgow and the Clyde towns which has made Loch Lomond (*below*) the best known of the Scottish freshwater lochs, but it is undoubtedly one of the most beautiful. The loch is the largest single stretch of fresh water in Great Britain, being twenty-four miles long and at its greatest width five miles. At its southern end Loch Lomond is dotted with numerous islands, on some of which are the ruins of former monastic buildings. From Balloch, at the foot of the loch, one can sail the full length to Ardlui. The road follows the western shore, passing through Luss, a village which boasts of being the prettiest in Scotland. The northern part of Loch Lomond is wild and lonely, and on the eastern shore the mountains reach down to the water. Towering above them all is Ben Lomond which is an easy climb from Inversnaid or Rowardennan. From the summit the view extends, on a clear day, over the whole of the estuary of the Clyde, to the mountains of Arran and to the Campsie Fells to the south-west of Stirling.

From Aberfoyle the Inversnaid road soon comes to Loch Ard (*upper right*), a charming lake surrounded by wooded slopes above which towers the peak of Ben Lomond. The road ascends the Pass of Aberfoyle, on the northern shore of the loch, and skirts the even more romantic Loch Chon, before joining the road which links Loch Lomond with Loch Katrine.

West of Aberfoyle the Menteith Hills look down on the Lake of Menteith, the only natural lake in Scotland which is not designated as a 'loch'. On one of the three islands in the lake stand the ruins of Inchmahome Priory, which was founded in the first half of the thirteenth century. Port of Menteith (*lower right*) is a modest little holiday resort on the north-eastern shore of the lake. The Menteith Hills are within the area of the Queen Elizabeth Forest Park which extends from the upper reaches of the River Forth to Loch Lomond.

Le Loch Lomond est sans doute un des plus beaux lacs de la Grande Bretagne. Près du Ross Point on jouit d'une belle vue sur le lac et sur les montagnes qui le dominent (*ci-contre*). Le Loch Ard (*ci-dessus*) se trouve à l'ouest d'Aberfoyle dans le Perthshire. C'est un lac charmant qui est entouré de collines boisées. Port of Menteith (*à gauche*), modeste centre de villégiature, est situé sur la rive nord du Lac de Menteith.

Der Loch Lomond ist nicht nur der größte, sondern auch einer der schönsten Seen von Großbritannien. In der Nähe von Ross Point hat man einen prächtigen Blick auf den See und die Berge (*gegenüber*). Der Loch Ard (*oben*), der sich westlich von Aberfoyle in Perthshire befindet, ist von Wäldern umringt, und in der Ferne sieht man den Gipfel des Ben Lomond. Port of Menteith (*links*) ist ein bescheidener Vergnügungsort an dem Ufer eines Sees, des Lake of Menteith.

Between Loch Katrine and Loch Achray (*below*) extends the incomparable region known as The Trossachs. The name has various interpretations, many holding, however, to that of 'bristly region' – in view of the afforestation which has been carried out in this area the name is undoubtedly an apt one. Most visitors come to The Trossachs from Aberfoyle, along the road built by the Duke of Montrose early last century and which is still called the Duke's Road. Loch Achray provided Turner with the subject of one of his well-known paintings. From the Trossachs Hotel on the northern bank the visitor may climb Ben A'an and will be rewarded by a grand view of the area.

North of Callander, a good centre for the exploration of The Trossachs and the surrounding region, the road to Killin first climbs over the Pass of Leny where the River Leny tumbles over a charming waterfall. On the far side of the pass is St Bride's Chapel, an ancient building which has been restored as a memorial to Sir Walter Scott. To the west lies Loch Voil (*lower right*) and its continuation Loch Doyne. Readers of Sir Walter Scott are familiar with the exploits of the outlaw Rob Roy, but some may be surprised to know that the romantic legends surround a man who did in fact exist, and his grave may be found in the roofless old church at Balquidder to the east of Loch Voil. Rob Roy MacGregor died at Inverlochlaraig some miles beyond the western end of the loch.

Strath Fillan (*upper right*) meets Glen Dochart and Glen Falloch at Crianlarich, an important road and rail junction. Three miles north-west of the town are the remains of St Fillan's Priory, a fourteenth-century foundation, by the side of a pool the waters of which were said to cure madness in those far-off days. The chapel bell may be seen in the National Museum of Antiquities at Edinburgh.

Les Trossachs s'étendent entre le Loch Katrine et le Loch Achray (*ci-contre*). Au nord de Callander, on trouve St Bride's Chapel. A l'ouest se trouvent les Lochs Voil (*ci-dessus, en bas*) et Doyne. La Strath Fillan (*ci-dessus, en haut*) rencontre le Glen Dochart et le Glen Falloch à Crianlarich. Au nord-ouest se dressent les ruines de St Fillan's Priory, datant du 14e siècle.

Zwischen Loch Katrine und Loch Achray (*gegenüber*) erstrecken sich die „Trossachs", eine einzigartige Landschaft. Eines von Turners wohlbekannten Gemälden hat Loch Achray zum Motiv. Westlich des Leny-Passes liegt Loch Voil (*oben*) und seine Fortsetzung, Loch Doyne. Bei Crianlarich stößt Strath Fillan (*ganz oben*) auf Glen Dochart und Glen Falloch.

St Fillan's (*ci-dessus*) est une petite plage à l'extrémité est du Loch Earn qui est particulièrement favorisée par des yachtmen. A l'autre bout du lac, près de Lochgoilhead, s'élève le Château d'Edinample qui date de la première moitié du 17e siècle. Au sud-est du Loch Tay (*à droite*) se trouve la ville de Killin, dominée par le Ben Lawers, le plus haut sommet du Perthshire. Le Loch Tummel (*ci-contre*) près de Pitlochry, offre une vue charmante.

St Fillan's (*oben*), ein kleiner Vergnügungsort am östlichen Ende des Loch Earn, ist bei Seglern besonders beliebt. Am anderen Ende steht das Schloß Edinample. Loch Tay (*rechts*), berühmt wegen seiner hervorragenden Forellen, ist ungefähr 25 km lang, bis 1,5 km breit und stellenweise an die 200 m tief. Von Queen's View, das seinen Namen 1866 anläßlich eines Besuches von Königin Viktoria erhielt, hat man einen schönen Blick auf Loch Tummel (*ganz rechts*).

Where the River Earn leaves Loch Earn is St Fillan's (*upper left*), a favourite resort of sailing enthusiasts and water skiers. At the western end of the six-mile-long loch is Lochearnhead, one of several places where Highland Games take place in summer. Edinample Castle, on the southern shore of Loch Earn, dates from the seventeenth century and is a good example of the Scottish Baronial style.

Loch Tay (*lower left*) which is well known for its excellent salmon and trout fishing, is about fifteen miles in length, up to a mile in width and attains a depth of over 500 feet. Killin, at its southwestern end, is a charming resort overlooked by Ben Lawers (3,984 feet), the highest mountain in Perthshire. The town is situated between the rivers Dochart and Lochay which join just before they enter Loch Tay. On the south bank of the Dochart in the grounds of Kinwell House are an ancient stone circle and one of the largest vines in Europe. The main road runs along the northern shore of Loch Tay, but the less frequented route on the south is recommended for it offers magnificent views along the whole of its length from Killin to Kenmore.

Few river valleys in the Highlands are lovelier than that of the Tummel, which is easily reached from Pitlochry, a most attractive holiday centre which has been a burgh since 1945 and since 1951 has had its own annual drama festival. Loch Tummel plays an important part in the hydro-electric development which has been carried out in the valley, and a completely new lake, Loch Faskally, has been created near Pitlochry. Salmon ladders up which the adult fish struggle to reach their spawning grounds, have been provided at both the dams. A beautiful prospect of Loch Tummel (*below*) is to be had from Queen's View, the name commemorating a visit by Queen Victoria in 1866. River and loch are framed in a woodland setting with the higher mountains to the north and west.

La route de Blairgowrie à Braemar, la plus haute de la Grande Bretagne, longe le Glen Shee (*ci-dessous, en haut*). La plupart des châteaux écossais sont construits dans le style des châteaux français. Glamis et Craigievar (*ci-dessous, en bas*) en sont deux exemples. Balmoral Castle (*ci-contre*) est une résidence royale construite en granit blanc dans le style écossais. Il se trouve sur une courbe de la Dee.

Das wunderbare Glen Shee (*unten*) liegt an der Straße von Blairgowrie nach Braemar, einer der höchsten Hauptstraßen Großbritanniens mit einem einzigartigen Ausblick. Vom Anfang des 17. Jahrhunderts stammen die Schlösser Glamis und Craigievar (*ganz unten*), die mit ihren vielen Türmen an französische Châteaux erinnern. Balmoral Castle (*gegenüber*) wurde in der zweiten Hälfte des vorigen Jahrhunderts gebaut.

The road from Blairgowrie to Braemar is not only the highest main road in Britain but is one of the finest scenic routes as well. It ascends beautiful Glen Shee (*upper left*), passing Spittal of Glenshee, once a hospice for travellers and now an hotel, and continues via the hairpin bends called the 'Devil's Elbow' over the Cairwell Pass into Aberdeenshire.

Many Scottish castles are reminiscent of French châteaux with rounded towers and many turrets. Good examples of the style are Glamis and Craigievar (*lower left*). The latter, which is situated six miles south of Alford, is seven storeys in height and has a fine hall with an enormous fireplace. It was built in the early part of the seventeenth century.

Deeside became 'Royal' in the second half of the last century when Balmoral Castle (*above*) was bought for Queen Victoria. She extended the estate by incorporating Ballochbuie Forest and left the Castle to her successors. Every year the Court is in residence at the Castle, which is built in typical Scottish style of white granite and has a fine situation on a curve of the River Dee in richly forested countryside. Although the Castle is not open to the public, the grounds may be visited on certain days in summer if the Court is not in residence. At Invercauld, some six miles beyond Balmoral, the picturesque 'Old Bridge of Dee' spans the river. This eighteenth-century bridge is now royal property and a new bridge has been built a short distance to the west.

Les Cairngorm Mountains, qui atteignent plus de 1230 m., sont granitiques. Le Loch Einich (*ci-dessus*) est au cœur de ces montagnes. La Spey (*à droite*) est la rivière la plus rapide de Grande-Bretagne et la plus longue d'Écosse. Le Strath Spey, sa partie basse, a donné son nom à une danse. Près d'Aviemore (*ci-contre*) un télésiège et un téléski montent dans les Cairngorms.

Mitten im Cairngorm Naturschutzpark liegt Loch Einich (*oben*), ein unwirtlicher Bergsee. Man kann ihn nur von Norden aus über Gleann Einich erreichen. Der Spey (*rechts*) ist einer der längsten Flüsse in Schottland, der reißendste in Großbritannien und berühmt wegen seines Lachses. In der Nähe von Aviemore (*gegenüber*) fahren eine Sesselbahn und ein Skilift in die Cairngorms.

There is little habitation in the Cairngorm Mountains, which exceed 4,000 feet in their highest peaks. They are composed of granite and their name has been given to beautiful crystals of brown or blue quartz which are known as cairngorms. Part of the area which includes Cairn Gorm Mountain has been designated the Glen More National Forest Park, while to the south of this region is the Cairngorm Nature Reserve where rare species of flora and fauna are to be found. Loch Einich (*upper left*), a wild and remote mountain lake, is situated in the heart of the Cairngorms. It is overlooked by the plateau known as Am Moine Mohr and is accessible only from the north along Gleann Einich. Ben Macdhui (4,296 feet) is the highest summit of the Cairngorm range.

The lower photograph on the opposite page is a view of the River Spey near Auchgourish. The Spey, one of the longest rivers in Scotland and the fastest flowing in Great Britain, is a noted salmon stream. The upper part of the Spey valley is followed by the main road and railway from Perth to Inverness. The road was first constructed by General Wade between 1726 and 1733, improved by Telford in 1830 and completely reconstructed a century later, so that it is now one of the finest mountain roads in the country. North of curiously named Boat of Garten we enter Strath Spey, the wide lower valley of the river which has given its name to one of the Highland dances.

Aviemore in Strath Spey has become the principal winter-sports resort in Scotland as well as an excellent centre for climbing in the Cairngorms. A newly constructed road leads eastwards skirting the northern side of Loch Morlich to Coire Cas from which a chair lift and ski lift (*below*) run to White Lady Shieling.

La route et le rail se côtoient de Fort William à Mallaig. D'abord depuis Corpach on découvre le Ben Nevis (*ci-dessus*), montagne volcanique qui s'élève à 1356 m. C'est le point culminant de la Grande Bretagne. De son sommet on peut voir les Cairngorms, les Hébrides et même parfois la côte irlandaise. En longeant le Loch Eil (*ci-contre, à droite*) on arrive à Glenfillan (*à droite*) avec le monument qui fut érigé en 1815, 70 ans après la révolte du Prince Charles.

Von Corpach aus hat man einen prächtigen Blick auf Ben Nevis (*oben*), den höchsten Berg Großbritanniens. Der Name Ben Nevis bedeutet „Berg der Nebel", da der Gipfel häufig von Wolken verhüllt wird. Von Corpach nach Mallaig geht die Landstraße an Loch Eil vorbei und erreicht Glenfillan (*rechts*). Hier erinnert ein Denkmal an den Aufstand von 1745, als der Stuart-Prinz und Thronprätendant Karl Eduard die schottischen Klans zu seinen Fahnen rief.

Fort William is an excellent centre for the exploration of the Western Highlands. It is named after William III, in whose reign the fort, originally built by General Monk during the Commonwealth, was reconstructed. From Fort William road and railway keep company westwards to Mallaig. Crossing the River Lochy and the Caledonian Canal we come first to Corpach from where there is an impressive view of Ben Nevis (*upper left*), the highest mountain in Great Britain, its summit being 4,406 feet above sea-level. Ben Nevis means the 'mountain of mists', as cloud frequently obscures the summit. It is a volcanic mountain whose northern rocky precipices are among the most imposing in Scotland and are certainly not for the inexperienced climber. From the summit the view ranges from the Cairngorms to the Hebrides and sometimes as far as the Irish coast.

The route now skirts Loch Eil (*below*), really an extension of Loch Linnhe to the west, and comes to Glenfinnan at the head of Loch Shiel. It was a minor skirmish in the valley of the Spean which heralded the '45 rebellion, but it was at Glenfinnan that Prince Charles raised his standard and summoned the clans to his cause. Over two thousand Highlanders rallied to him, and his forces gained early spectacular successes. He was acclaimed at Edinburgh, won the Battle of Prestonpans, crossed the border and reached Derby. Returning to Scotland he was pursued by the Duke of Cumberland and was at length defeated at Culloden. Although his army was butchered, Charles Edward escaped and eventually returned to France. The monument at Glenfinnan (*lower left*), standing close to where the River Finnan flows into the loch, was erected seventy years after the rebellion. It is in the care of the National Trust for Scotland. From Glenfinnan road and railway continue to Mallaig, from where there are regular ferry services to Skye and other islands of the Hebrides, including the quaintly named Eigg (pronounced Egg) and Rum. The ships which cross the Sound of Sleat are the only means of transport between the Western Isles and the mainland and are essential for the continued prosperity of the Islanders.

The whole of the north-west of Scotland is divided from the rest by the Great Glen, a natural rift containing three lochs – Lochy, Oich and Ness. The Caledonian Canal makes use of these lochs, and although little used today it remains a remarkable example of marine engineering. Loch Lochy, the most southerly of the three, is enclosed by steep wooded hillsides. It is ten miles long and a mile wide. The River Arkaig connects Loch Lochy with Loch Arkaig. The road connecting the two is known as the 'Dark Mile', because of the interlacing of the trees bordering the highway.

Loch Ness (*upper right*) is twenty-four miles in length, about a mile wide and reaches a depth of 700 feet. The modern road follows the western shore, the road on the east side of the loch having been built by General Wade in the eighteenth century. Loch Ness is famous for its 'monster'; many believe in the existence of this creature, and claims are even made for authentic photographs of the loch's famous inhabitant. Whether one is a believer or a sceptic there is no doubt that the denizen of the loch is good for trade! On the western shore, not far from Drumnadrochit, are the ruins of Castle Urquhart (*lower right*). There was a previous stronghold here which was captured in the twelfth century by Edward I who reconstructed the Castle. At the southern end of Loch Ness is the town of Fort Augustus. The Fort was built in 1715, captured by the Jacobites in '45 and retaken after Culloden.

Loch Oich (*below*), the smallest of the three lakes, is about four miles in length. About half-way along its western shore is Invergarry from which a beautiful road ascends Glen Garry to the coast. Invergarry Castle, burnt down by the Duke of Cumberland after Culloden, was the refuge of Bonnie Prince Charlie both before and after the battle.

Trois grands lacs, les Loch Ness, Oich et Lochy, s'étendent le long du Great Glen qui parcoure les Highlands. Le Loch Ness (*ci-dessus, en haut*), long de 35 km., est célèbre pour son monstre. On notera à l'ouest Castle Urquhart et Fort Augustus au sud. Au bord du Loch Oich (*ci-contre*) se trouve Invergarry Castle.

Im Great Glen befinden sich drei Seen: Loch Ness, Loch Oich und Loch Lochy. Loch Ness (*ganz oben*) ist nahezu 35 km lang, 1,5 km breit und bis zu 20 m tief. Berühmt ist er vor allem wegen seines sagenumwobenen Untiers. Am westlichen Ufer steht das Scholß Urquhart (*oben*). An Loch Oich (*links*), dem kleinsten der Seen, findet man Schloß Invergarry.

Inverness est la ville principale des Highlands du Nord. Son château (*ci-dessous, en haut*) date due 19ᵉ siècle mais est bâti sur le site d'anciens châteaux. Le Glen Cannich (*ci-contre*) a été barré au niveau des Lochs Mullardoch et Lungard pour fournir de l'hydro-éléctricité. Le Glen Affric (*ci-dessous, en bas*), au sud du Glen Cannich, est aussi pittoresque; le Loch Affric est dominé par des montagnes majestueuses.

Inverness ist das Zentrum der nördlichen Highlands. Das Schloß (*unten*) stammt in seiner jetzigen Form aus dem 19. Jahrhundert, hat aber an derselben Stelle viele Vorgänger gehabt. Die Landschaft des Glen Cannich (*rechts*) ist von einer grandiosen Schönheit. Je weiter man ins Tal vorstößt, desto romantischer wird die Szenerie. In Glen Affric (*ganz unten*) genießt man eine ähnliche, romantische Landschaft.

Inverness is the principal town of the Northern Highlands and has much of interest. On Castle Hill the present Castle (*upper left*) serves as the County Offices. The present building is of nineteenth-century date, but stands on the site of several former castles. The Town Cross incorporates a rough stone known as the 'Stone of the Tubs', on which it is said women used to rest their pots on returning from filling them at the river. St Andrews' Cathedral, on the western bank of the Ness, is a handsome building in Decorated style.

Glen Cannich (*above*) is reached from Beauly or Inverness by following the course of the Beauly River – or River Glass – to its confluence with the River Cannich. The scenery in the glen is particularly attractive and becomes more and more wildly romantic in the upper part of the valley, where Lochs Mullardoch and Lungard have been harnessed to provide hydro-electric power.

Glen Affric (*lower left*) lies to the south of Glen Connich to which it is connected by a tunnel aqueduct. The scenery in this glen is as wild and majestic as that of its northern neighbour. The level of Loch Benevean in Glen Affric was raised when the hydro-electric scheme was constructed and this resulted in a number of small islands being formed. Further along the glen is Loch Affric which is overlooked by mountains approaching 4,000 feet in height. Walkers, but not vehicles, can go on and reach Loch Duich in Ross and Cromarty.

Skye est l'île la plus importante des Hébrides Intérieures. Du Broadfoot Bay on embrasse une belle vue des « Red Hills » (ci-dessus). La côte du Wester Ross est découpée par une série de lochs de mer, tels que les Lochs Ewe, Carron et Torridon (à droite) qui sont entourés de hautes montagnes. Le petit port d'Ullapool (ci-contre), fondé à la fin du 18e siècle pour faire avancer la pêche aux harengs, est aujourd'hui un excellent centre pour la Haute Écosse.

Skye, die Hauptinsel der Inneren Hebriden, ist so von Buchten durchzogen, daß man an keinem Punkt auf ihr weiter als 8 km vom Meer entfernt ist. Von Broadfoot Bay aus hat man einen schönen Blick auf die „Red Hills" (oben). Upper Loch Torridon führt nach Glen Torridon, einem von hohen Bergen umgebenen Tal. Am Ende des 18. Jahrhunderts wurde Ullapool (ganz rechts) gegründet, um die Heringfischerei zu fördern. Heute ist es auch ein beliebter Ferienort.

Skye, often called the 'misty isle', for the craggy summits of the Cuillin Mountains are often wreathed in mist, is the principal island of the Inner Hebrides. Skye is fringed with sea-lochs which divide the island into a number of peninsulas and no point is more than five miles from the sea. The scenery is without doubt unsurpassed anywhere in the British Isles and thousands of visitors cross from the mainland every year. From Broadford Bay, about eight miles west of the Kyle of Lochalsh, there are impressive views of the Red Hills (*upper left*), of which the highest peaks exceed 2,300 feet. The way of life of the people of Skye has changed but little through the ages, and the crofter's cottage is a symbol of the independent yet friendly character of the islanders. The capital is Portree, a name which recalls a visit paid to the island by James V. Dr. Johnson and Boswell visited Skye in 1773 and their enthusiasm for the beauty of the island has since been shared by countless others who have made the crossing from Mallaig or from the Kyle of Lochalsh.

The coast of Wester Ross is indented by a series of fine sea-lochs, of which the largest are Loch Ewe, Loch Carron and Loch Torridon. The last-named consists of a wide estuary and Upper Loch Torridon (*lower left*) which gives access to Glen Torridon, to the north of which rises Liathach, one of Scotland's finest mountains. It consists of steep terraces of Torridon sandstone with a striking corrie on the northern side. These sandstone peaks, often topped with white quartzite, present an almost theatrical quality when the setting sun falls on them, and they form a most lovely background to the waters of the lochs.

At the end of the eighteenth century the port of Ullapool (*below*) was founded by the Fisheries Association to give impetus to the herring industry. Today it is also an excellent base from which to explore the Western Highlands. The little township is beautifully situated on the northern shore of Loch Broom; on the far side of the loch rises Ben Goleach, the highest point of the peninsula separating Loch Broom from Little Loch Broom.

Sutherland, in the extreme north-west of Scotland, extends across the country from the Atlantic to the North Sea. The northern and western regions are without doubt the wildest and most unspoiled parts of the Highlands, and not even the advent of hydro-electric schemes can seriously challenge Nature in her own domain. The present population of Sutherland, fifth in size of the Scottish counties, is only some 13,000 and Dornoch, the county town, had less than a thousand inhabitants at the last census. Of the many lochs in the county Loch Assynt (*above*) is overlooked by the bare peaks of grey gneiss. At the southern end of the loch is Inchnadamph, a small fishing resort, near which are the ruins of Ardvreck Castle, dating from the fifteenth century.

East of Cape Wrath are three major inlets of the sea, the Kyle of Durness, Loch Eriboll and the Kyle of Tongue. Loch Eriboll bites deep into the Sutherland mountains. Its western shore is guarded by Whiten Head, seen (*upper right*) with Sangobeg Bay and the entrance to Eriboll Bay. Loch Eriboll provides a safe anchorage for shipping.

Dunrobin Castle (*lower right*), just north of Golspie on the eastern coast of Sutherland, is set in a fine park on a terrace overlooking the sea. The original castle was much smaller than the present buildings, considerable additions and restorations having taken place. The original square keep was built in the latter part of the thirteenth century but the present facade is only a century old. The gardens are notable for their flowers, and the park contains a museum where local archaeological finds are exhibited.

Le Sutherland se situe à l'extrême nord-ouest de l'Écosse et sa population n'est que de 13000 habitants. Dornoch, la capitale, en renferme moins de 1000. C'est la région la plus sauvage, malgré l'apparition des barrages. Le Loch Assynt (*ci-contre*) est typique de la région. A l'est du Cap Wrath s'étendent les Kyles de la Durness et de la Tongue at le Loch Eriboll, limité à l'ouest par la Whiten Head (*ci-dessous, en haut*) et la baie de Sangobeg. Dunrobin Castle (*ci-dessous, en bas*) fut d'abord construit au 13e siècle.

Sutherland im Nordwesten Schottlands erstreckt sich quer durch die Insel vom Atlantik bis zur Nordsee. Von Loch Assynt aus hat man einen eindrucksvollen Blick auf die kahlen Berge der Landschaft von Sutherland (*gegenüber*). Loch Eriboll ist eine der drei größten Buchten östlich von Kap Wrath; das Westufer wird vom Berg Whiten Head beherrscht (*unten*). Der älteste erhaltene Teil von Schloß Dunrobin (*ganz unten*) stammt aus dem 13. Jahrhundert; die gegenwärtige Fassade ist jedoch nur 100 Jahre ait.

Helmsdale (*à gauche, dessus*) est un petit port de pêche sur la côte ouest du Sutherland. Dans son château, qui date du 15ᵉ siècle, le comte et la comtesse de Sutherland furent empoisonnés en 1567 par la comtesse de Caithness. A l'est de John o' Groats, à l'extrémité nord-ouest de l'Écosse on trouve le Duncansby Head (*à gauche, dessous*).

Helmsdale (*links, oben*) ist ein kleiner Fischerhafen an der Westküste von Sutherland. In seinem Schloß fand 1567 ein Doppelmord statt, als der Graf und die Gräfin von Sutherland von der Gräfin von Caithness ermordet wurden. Östlich von John o' Groats, im nordöstlichen Winkel des Landes befindet sich Duncansby Head (*links unten*).

The coastal road from Sutherland leads eastwards into Caithness and comes to Thurso and John o' Groats, traditionally though not strictly accurately the most northerly point of Great Britain. It is the terminus or starting-point of many contests for motorists, cyclists and even pedestrians seeking to cover the 876 miles to Land's End in Cornwall. From John o' Groats there are fine views to seaward of Stroma Island and the Orkneys, while still farther north lie the Shetlands, a group of more than a hundred islands, notable for their fine cliff scenery. To the east of John o' Groats is the headland of Duncansby (*lower photograph*) with the three detached stacks just off shore. Sixteen miles to the south of John o' Groats lies the ancient borough of Wick with a harbour which was designed by Telford. A mile to the south of the town the ruins of a castle, known locally as the 'Old Man of Wick', stand on the edge of the cliffs, providing a prominent landmark for sailors.

Helmsdale (*upper photograph*) is in Sutherland, just over the Caithness border. Early in the nineteenth century the interior of Sutherland was 'cleared' of most of its population who were forced to move to more prosperous areas, and Helmsdale was one of the places where some of the displaced families were resettled. Helmsdale Castle, dating from the late fifteenth century, was the scene of a double murder in 1567 when the Earl and Countess of Sutherland were poisoned by the Countess of Caithness.

85306 350 8

© *Copyright 1972 Jarrold & Sons Ltd, Norwich, England*
Published and printed in Great Britain by Jarrold & Sons Ltd, Norwich, England. 372